I Like Winter

Learning the ER Sound

Greg Moskal

Phonics
for the
REAL World™

Rosen Classroom Books and Materials™
New York

Winter starts in December.

December

Sunday	Monday	Tuesday	Wednesday	Thursday	Friday	Saturday
1	2	3	4	5	6	7
8	9	10	11	12	13	14
15	16	17	18	19	20	21
22	23	24	25	26	27	28
29	30	31				3

Winter weather can be cold and snowy.

It is fun to play outside in winter.

I never go outside without my winter boots.

I always wear my winter hat.

I make a snowman with my older sister.

I throw snowballs with
my sisters.

We go sledding with our mother
and father.

I go inside when it is time for dinner.

I like winter. Do you?

Word List

December

dinner

father

mother

never

older

sister

weather

winter

Instructional Guide

Note to Instructors:

One of the essential skills that enable a young child to read is the ability to associate letter-sound symbols and blend these sounds to form words. Phonics instruction can teach children a system that will help them decode unfamiliar words and, in turn, enhance their word-recognition skills. We offer a phonics-based series of books that are easy to read and understand. Each book pairs words and pictures that reinforce specific phonetic sounds in a logical sequence. Topics are based on curriculum goals appropriate for early readers in the areas of science, social studies, and health.

Letter/Sound: er – Pronounce and write the following words: *number, winter, after, better, under, answer, water, weather, flower, summer.* Have the child underline the **er** in each word and talk about the sound these letters make.

- Have the child copy the following words on index cards: *her, serve, enter, under, sister, every, zipper, sticker, were, spider, verb.* Ask the child to read them and underline the **er** in each word. Have the child sort words according to those that have **er** in the middle position of the word and those that have **er** in the ending position of the word. Ask them to use the words in sentences.

Phonics Activities: List the following words: *help, hit, read, jump, teach, drive, sing, dance, dive, play, travel.* Lead the child to classify the words as action words. Ask: "How can we change the action word *help* into a name word?" Add **er** to change *help* to *helper.* Continue in the same way with the remaining words. Have the child underline **er** in each word and use the word in a sentence.

- Provide the child with two response cards, one for **ar**, one for **er**. Have them hold up the appropriate card as you write and pronounce words, such as the following: *car, father, barn, under, dark, water, arm, zipper, garden, mother, farm, never,* etc. List the words in two columns. Have the child underline **ar** or **er** in each word.

- Have the child find the **er** word in the following sentence: *I'm the best hitter on my baseball team.* Ask them to write sentences using **er** words from the phonics activities above. Have the child read their sentences to you.

Additional Resources:

- Burke, Jennifer S. *Cold Days.* Danbury, CT: Children's Press, 2000.
- Fowler, Allan. *How Do You Know It's Winter?* Danbury, CT: Children's Press, 1991.
- Saunders-Smith, Gail. *Warm Clothes.* Danbury, CT: Children's Press, 1998.
- Schaefer, Lola M. *Cold Day.* Mankato, MN: Capstone Press, Inc., 2000.

Published in 2002 by The Rosen Publishing Group, Inc.
29 East 21st Street, New York, NY 10010

Book Design: Ron A. Churley

Photo Credits: Cover © Richard Price/FPG International; pp. 3, 9, 19 by Ron A. Churley; p. 5 © Telegraph Colour Library/FPG International; p. 7 © VCG/FPG International; p. 11 © Dorian Weber/Index Stock; p. 13 © Bob Winsett/Index Stock; p. 15 © It Stock International/Index Stock; p. 17 © Table Mesa Prod./Index Stock; p. 21 © Kent Default/Index Stock.

Library of Congress Cataloging-in-Publication Data

Moskal, Greg, 1971-
  I like winter : learning the ER sound / Greg Moskal. — 1st ed.
     p. cm. — (Power phonics/phonics for the real world)
  ISBN 0-8239-5939-2 (lib. bdg.)
  ISBN 0-8239-8284-X (pbk.)
  6 pack ISBN 0-8239-9252-7
  1. Winter—Juvenile literature. 2. Reading—Phonetic method—Juvenile literature. 3. English language—Phonetics—Juvenile literature.
  [1. Winter.] I. Title. II. Series.
  QB637.8 .M68 2002
  508.2—dc21
                                                    2001001132

Manufactured in the United States of America